Pathfinder 13

A CILT series for language teachers

Continuous assessment and recording

John Thorogood

CiLT

Other titles in the PATHFINDER series:

Reading for pleasure in a foreign language (Ann Swarbrick)
Yes - but will they behave? Managing the interactive classroom (Susan Halliwell)
On target - teaching in the target language (Susan Halliwell and Barry Jones)
Communication re-activated: teaching pupils with learning difficulties (Bernardette Holmes)
Bridging the gap: GCSE to 'A' level (John Thorogood and Lid King)
Making the case for languages (Alan Moys and Richard Townsend)
Languages home and away (Alison Taylor)
Being creative (Barry Jones)
Departmental planning and schemes of work (Clive Hurren)
Progressing through the Attainment Targets (Ian Lane)
Fair enough? Equal opportunities and modern languages (Vee Harris)

Acknowledgements

To Michael Dennison, for his support in the work of the Oxford Schools Programmes of Study team. Also to the members of that team for developing the model used in this book.

First published 1992
Copyright © 1992 Centre for Information on Language Teaching and Research
ISBN 1 874016 02 X

Cover by Logos Design & Advertising
Printed in Great Britain by Oakdale Printing Co. Ltd.

Published by Centre for Information on Language Teaching and Research, Regent's College, Inner Circle, Regent's Park, London NW1 4NS.

All rights reserved. No part of the publication may be reproduced, stored in a retrieval system, or transmitted in any form or by any means, electronic, mechanical, photocopying, recording, or otherwise, without the prior permission of the Copyright owner.

Contents

		Page
Introduction		1
1.	A point of departure	2
2.	National Curriculum assessment and recording requirements	10
3.	Involving pupils in their own assessment and recording	15
4.	Coping with continuous assessment	18
5.	Recording pupils' performance	24
6.	Reporting progress through a periodic review sheet	27
7.	Recapitulation and conclusions	30

Introduction

Despite its unpoetic title, *Recording progress* (Pathfinder 1) enjoyed great popularity. This has reflected the keenness of many teachers of modern languages to get to grips with the exacting task of assessing continuously and recording their pupils' progress as required by the National Curriculum. Although that book described a system which had been initiated before there was any talk of a National Curriculum, there was instant recognition that the system embodied National Curriculum principles.

As a result of many in-service training talks in which I discussed how the more specific requirements of the National Curriculum framework might be handled at the recording stage, I have decided to write this sequel to *Recording progress*. In it, I shall briefly reiterate those principles of recording which still hold good, and demonstrate the workings of the system originally adopted to implement those principles. Thereafter, I propose to reflect on the likely implications of the National Curriculum for continuous assessment and then to suggest ways in which this probable scenario can be handled administratively.

The essence of my argument is the importance of integrating the process of planning, teaching and assessment. Teachers should never lose sight of the fact that they have always prepared, taught, marked, kept a mark book and reported on progress. In principle, the National Curriculum asks little more of them than this…

1. A point of departure

Examples of helpful practice in recent years

In *Recording progress*, I identified some recent developments in the assessment and recording of pupils' progress in modern languages which had provided helpful models for the development of a departmental system in a large comprehensive school.

- Defined topic-based syllabuses had become a reality with Graded Objectives in Modern Languages (GOML) schemes in almost every Local Education Authority and an emergent GCSE modular course with defined assessment activities for each module. This had proved an agreeable departure from syllabuses so laconic as to mean nothing to the uninitiated. It was a significant step towards integrating syllabus planning with assessment and informing the learner about past or future work.

- Pupil profiling provided a departure from off-the-cuff generalisations about past performance and showed the way to structured statements with appropriate prompt headings. Conventional reporting systems had provided little space for the conscientious teacher to give a full and balanced account of a pupil's progress and offered no supportive framework (e.g. checklists) for reporting consistently on relevant features of performance (e.g. skills, accuracy). On the contrary, they favoured bland and non-committal platitudes.

- Levels of attainment had replaced marks out of an arbitrary total to give **positive** recognition of achievement and these levels were **related to agreed criteria**. Previously, *marks out of...* had highlighted pupils' failure rather than their success and had often been idiosyncratically practised without reference to any yardstick of performance.

- Communicative assessment tasks were beginning to be used to assess performance, putting emphasis on the pupil's ability to achieve a practical end or make an informed decision on the basis of his or her understanding of the language performance. Assessment on the principle of *did they or didn't they get what they wanted* had made the marking process much easier.

- Continuous assessment in its real sense, i.e. of counting day-to-day performance towards pupils' level of attainment, had been foreshadowed by the periodic testing procedures of the graded objectives schemes. Assessment by summative examination alone had focused unfairly on pupils' performance on a randomly picked day in their life and sampled poorly both their characteristic performance and the content of the syllabus studied.

Both the good practice explicit in these new approaches and the inadequacies implicit in their neglect led us to formulate a number of guiding principles and to make some assumptions about our assessment and recording procedure which would embody these principles.

Principles of effective recording of assessment

- Teaching and assessment should be integrated at the planning stage to ensure that pupils and teachers could look forward with certainty to what would be taught and therefore assessed at each stage of the learning process.

- Assessment should be task-based - that is, pupils should be assessed on pre-communicative linguistic exercises, not purely on the accuracy with which they used the language, but on a broader view of whether their linguistic performance in all its aspects would have achieved the user's aims. This makes the achievement easier to assess and record, because one is asking the simple question 'Did they do it or didn't they?' rather than the more conventional 'How perfectly did they do it?'. The degree of linguistic accuracy and appropriateness required will be determined by the task itself, through the specified relationship or setting.

- Assessment should be by levels, stressing the positive ('This is how far you have come in the last year - well done!') rather than by 'marks out of' which implied degrees of failure. These levels should be defined by criteria, so that teachers could be guided in their selection or design of appropriate assessment activities and so that pupils and others could have access to the meaning of each level of performance.

- Assessment would be on a continuous basis whereby teachers would record any measurable attainment or increment in attainment as and when the pupil furnished evidence of it. Tasks and activities assessed would in most cases tend to occur naturally as classwork or homework in the day-to-day learning process.

Assumptions

In the light of these agreed principles it was assumed that:

★ Teachers and pupils would be helped in planning their teaching and learning if there existed a document setting out the communicative aims of each unit of study which could also act as a pupil's record of achievement or profile. This document would be available to pupils at the beginning of a unit and would be kept by them as an on-going record (figure 1).

KING ALFRED'S SCHOOL WANTAGE, MODERN LANGUAGES DEPARTMENT
1ST YEAR GERMAN COURSE. MODULE D1.4

Pupil's Name:	Tutor:	Language Teacher

In town: shops and shopping

Description of achievement	Level reached				TEACHER'S COMMENTS AND ADVICE
	1	2	3	4	
I can read and understand a shopping list given me by a German friend					
I can understand brief information on departments and special offers in a store.					
I can understand what I am asked to go and buy.					
..and short announcements in a store					
I can buy a range of items in food, clothing and tourist shops.					
...or ask someone to get them for me.					
Make a shopping list for my German friend.					
Design a poster for a German shop window.					

GRAMMAR CHECKLIST	taught	understood

STUDY SKILLS

How I conduct myself in class
How I cope with homework
How I present my written work

PUPIL'S COMMENTS
What you found most interesting/enjoyable. What you found difficult. Any remarks on things you did which have some connection with German or Germany (e.g. visits/films etc.)

Figure 1

★ Study programmes would be topic-based.

★ All recorded assessment would be by levels defined by agreed criteria (figure 2) and these criteria would be expressed in a way which would inform teachers in their choice of assessment material.

CHART OF CRITERIA FOR PERFORMANCE TASKS IN MODERN LANGUAGES. OCEA

		Level 1	Level 2	Level 3	Level 4
LISTENING		OUTCOME Has understanding of individual words	OUTCOME Has understanding of short items/key words of text	OUTCOME Can explain what text is about	OUTCOME Can give a detailed summary in English
		TEXT Short, self-contained, delivered at a comprehensible speed Using recently acquired vocabulary and structures	TEXT Possibly longer and more difficult	TEXT Sustained (e.g. 50-75 w) delivered at a faster speed than L1/2. Possible background noise and wider range of known vocabulary/structures	TEXT As L3 but 75w + + possible regional accent + more abstract content + inclusion of unfamiliar vocabulary/structure
		TASK Questions relating to individual words and with element of guidance. Could include grid filling. 1 detail per utterance	TASK As for 1, but... requires understanding of relationship between words Up to 2/3 details extracted per utterance	TASK As in 1 and 2, + Questions require an element of summary - some guidance given on organisation of material.	TASK Questions require unguided organisation of ideas in the text and ability to draw conclusions/express opinions/infer meanings of new words
READING		OUTCOME Has understanding of individual words	OUTCOME Has understanding of short items/key words of text	OUTCOME Can explain what text is about	OUTCOME Can give a detailed summary in English
		TEXT Short, self-contained, printed text or very clear authentic h/writing	TEXT Possibly longer or more difficult	TEXT Sustained (e.g. 50-75 w) inc. less clear authentic h/writing + wider range of known structures	TEXT As L3 but 75w + + more abstract content + inclusion of unknown vocabulary/structure
		TASK As for Listening above	TASK As for Listening above	TASK As for Listening above	TASK As for Listening above
WRITING		OUTCOME Can produce single recognisable words and phrases.	OUTCOME Can produce short notes and simple sentences in comprehensible French	OUTCOME Can produce more continuous text showing such grammatical competence as is necessary for communication.	OUTCOME As for L3, but grammatical competence such that little or no effort is required of the reader. Evidence of a wider range of vocabulary and idiom than at L3. Learner should be able to express opinions/attitudes and negotiate.

Source: Oxford Certificate of Educational Achievement (OCEA)

Figure 2

★ Assessment would be continuous and would replace such periodic testing as end of year exams.

★ Teachers would maintain a version of the traditional mark book as a group record, but it would be ruled to give emphasis to the communicative tasks specified in the pupils' own records or profiles (figure 3).

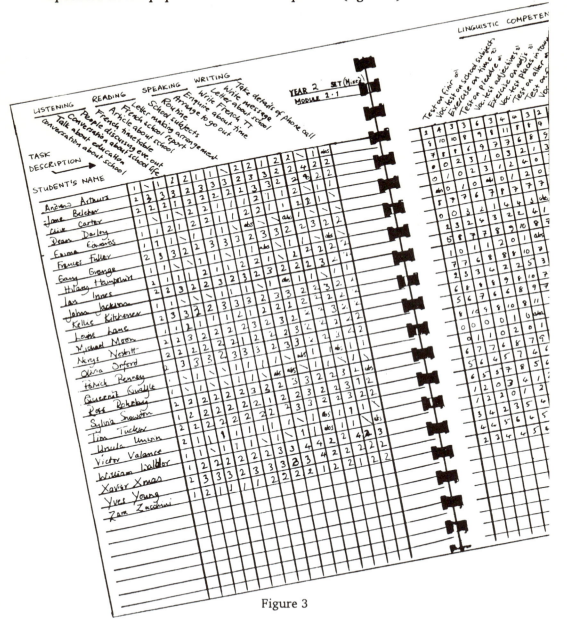

Figure 3

★ A school review sheet (figure 4) for external reporting would accommodate recorded levels of achievement for each unit studied to date, together with space for teacher's and pupil's respective reactions to the year's progress and for a parental response.

KING ALFRED'S SCHOOL MODERN LANGUAGES REVIEW SHEET

Date of review	Student's name	Teacher	Tutor
12/6/90	Gary Grange	JRT.	SD. Form 2SD

Language: French.

Summary of achievement in modules completed

Module No. 2·1	Module Title: Places / Travel / Arriving in a French Home			
Skill	Listen	Read	Speak	Write
Level	3	3	3	3.
Module No. 2·2	Module Title: Visiting a French friend's school			
Skill	Listen	Read	Speak	Write
Level	3	3	3	2.
Module No. 2·3	Module Title: Spending money – Presents & Snacks.			
Skill	Listen	Read	Speak	Write
Level	2	3	3	3.

Diagnostic grading as appropriate.

Pronunciation	B
Accent/intonation	C
Spelling	B
Grammatical Concepts	B
Self-reliance in studies	A.

Student's self-assessment and reactions to the course.

I have enjoyed the work this year, especially the role-play in pairs and groups. I sometimes worry about verb tests, because I don't always understand why verbs change the way they do! Module 2·3 was really useful when we went to Erquy in May. G. Grange.

Teacher's assessment

You have maintained a high standard through hard work and enthusiasm in classwork. In spite of occasional inaccuracies in writing, you communicate well. If your lower listening score this term bothers you, I can copy you an interesting practice tape. Jim Teacher.

Parents' response to assessment

We are really relieved that Gary has enjoyed his French this year after his anxieties in the 1st Year. How can we support him in his work? Marian Grange.

Figure 4

The complete system is illustrated by the diagram in figure 5.

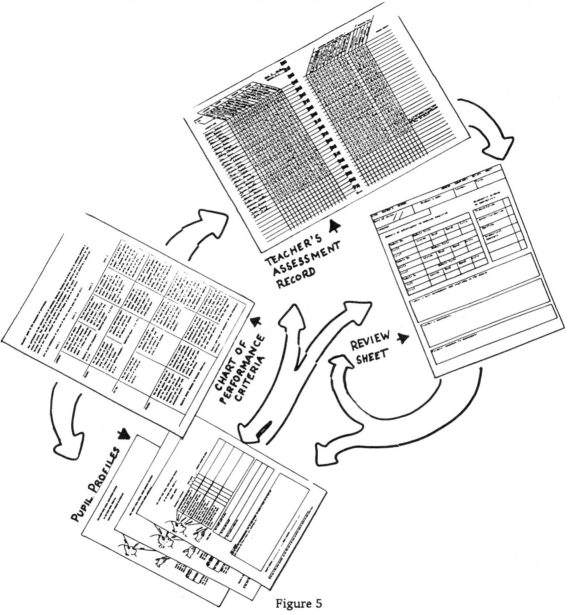

Figure 5

Reflections on the system as summarised

Upon reading the relevant documents we find that the principles underlying the system described in *Recording progress* foreshadowed the following essential requirements of the National Curriculum framework for modern foreign languages:

- continuous assessment;

- attainment measured by levels;

- levels defined by criteria (statements of attainment);

- the keeping of records of attainment;

- reporting of progress on a regular basis.

This system could therefore be offered as a template for National Curriculum assessment and recording after appropriate modifications. Under the National Curriculum we must take account of the following important developments:

★ Continuous assessment will be subject to some form of moderation - to be made more explicit by the School Examinations and Assessment Council (SEAC) in the near future.

★ The continuous assessment process will be further moderated by the standard assessment tasks (SATs) to be set (probably for the most part externally) at the end of key stage 3 and as GCSE or in some other form at the end of key stage 4.

★ There are ten levels of attainment in the National Curriculum.

★ The criteria for the National Curriculum are differently conceived from those used in former graded systems of assessment and are likely to be more numerous (102 in all).

★ The foregoing will need to be accommodated in the design and layout of any recording documentation.

★ Reporting of progress will acquire a statutory dimension over and above the good intentions of any school in wishing to keep various interested parties informed of pupils' progress.

2. National Curriculum assessment and recording requirements

What is so far known about National Curriculum assessment requirements?

Pupils will be subject not only to continuous assessment in the classroom but to standard assessment tasks (SATs), which will be taken as examinations at the end of each key stage. Since at the time of writing we do not know what form the modern language SATs will take, they will not be our concern in this book. However, it must be the hope of language teachers that SATs will be able to reflect in some way the variety of assessment techniques which teachers will use for continuous assessment during the relevant key stage. The tests will have to be simple and economical to administer and to moderate. Given that the test will probably be a fairly crude measure but that the results will be of great significance to learners, parents and the school, it is perhaps all the more important that teachers are in a position to diagnose fully the achievements of their pupils.

Allusion to assessment in the various statutory and non-statutory documents is sparse and varies between the laconic and the very general. In the Section 4 Order, § 22, it is stated (my emphasis):

> The Secretary of State has decided that:
>
> as to Key Stage 3
>
> - assessment should combine **teachers' own judgments based on ordinary classroom work** and the results of standard tests which will be administered by teachers.

and in § 24:

> Bearing in mind the likely future statutory requirements and the need, meanwhile, to keep pupils and parents appraised of progress, **teachers are strongly encouraged to make arrangements from the outset informally to assess, and record, their pupils' attainments**. In doing so they should have regard to the requirements of the Order under Section 4(2)(a) and (b) of the Act, so as:
>
> i. to ensure that individual pupils are acquiring the knowledge and understanding which enable them to work at appropriate levels for any given attainment target and programme of study;

> ii. to inform those with an interest - notably parents, or other teachers with either current or imminent responsibility for the pupil - about individual pupils' progress; and
>
> iii. to build up a record of evidence of each pupil's attainments, which may include examples of work, as a basis for future judgments about the levels reached at the end of a key stage.

The non-statutory guidance (NSG) gives what it describes as 'interim guidance on assessment issues', but is obliged to leave the whole issue of continuous teacher assessment to the School Examinations and Assessment Council (SEAC) which in the words of the NSG will be producing an anthology of 'Pupils' work assessed'. In addition to any future SEAC guidance which is specific to modern languages, the reader is recommended to obtain from SEAC its existing publications on assessment at key stage 3 of which *Teacher assessment in practice* in particular imparts the spirit in which continuous assessment for the National Curriculum might be conducted. This book identifies three central issues:

- assessing as part of teaching and learning;
- involving pupils in their own assessment;
- collecting evidence and recording attainment.

A modern languages-specific booklet from SEAC is now in existence and will have reached schools by the time this book is available. It deals with five issues related to assessment and has a useful aide-mémoire page which lists the five issues with questions to get you thinking about what provision you are making.

The issues are as for *Teacher assessment in practice* with, in addition:

- professional judgment;
- reporting.

The booklet is called *Teacher assessment at key stage 3 - modern foreign languages* (ref: A/038/L/92) and is obtainable, should you require additional copies, from:

Schools Examinations and Assessment Council
Newcombe House
Notting Hill Gate
London W11 3JB

The scheme summarised in Chapter 1 goes a long way towards addressing the first of the issues identified by SEAC, i.e. assessing as part of teaching and learning, insofar as the design of the pupil profile entails an integrated approach at the initial planning stage.

A programme-led approach to assessment/recording

The appearance of the National Curriculum language documents and their many recommendations on planning programmes of study has led to teachers adopting a programme-led rather than an assessment-led approach to the process of recording progress. Since the experience of developing the Oxford Certificate of Educational Achievement (OCEA) style of recording system, I have been fortunate in having the opportunity to work with a group of middle school teachers engaged in drawing up a joint National Curriculum key stage 3 programme of study to ensure standardisation and continuity for the middle school to upper school transfer. Equipped with the insights provided by the *Final report*, we worked along the following lines.

The first step was to list topics which participating teachers had experience in teaching through the target language (which in this case was exclusively French). We established a progression on the basis of 'widening circles of experience' (figure 6).

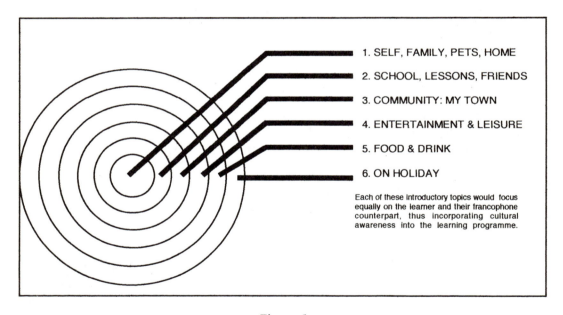

Figure 6

From this there evolved a year-planning chart (figure 7) to present in visual form the combination of progression between units (the vertical dimension) and progression through units (the horizontal dimension).

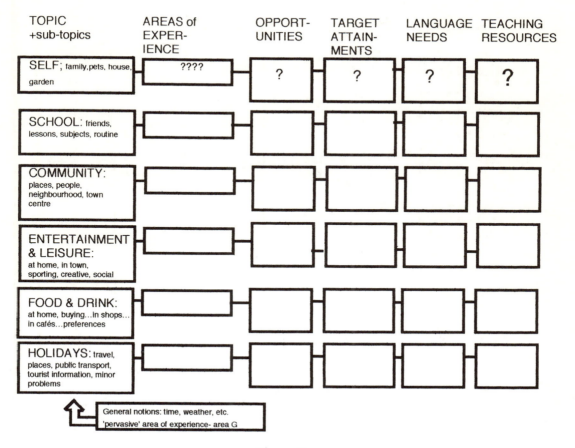

Figure 7

The issue of progression through a unit gave rise to a unit-planning chart which was used to ensure a logical planning procedure. This chart (figure 8) starts with the unit topic. From this topic, sub-topics are derived, enabling the unit to be broken down into manageable stages. For each sub-topic, and here we were instantly reminded of the close link between teaching and assessment, a number of target tasks were identified and listed alongside that sub-topic. These would provide the objectives of the unit. The performance of each communicative task would require mastery of certain linguistic items which were listed in the next column (note that under 'vocabulary' the idea was not to include compendious word lists, but merely to indicate categories such as 'things to order at a restaurant', 'adjectives for physical appearance', etc). The final column listed teaching resources which might be suitable for teaching the sub-topics and language and providing the target tasks, whether for practice or assessment.

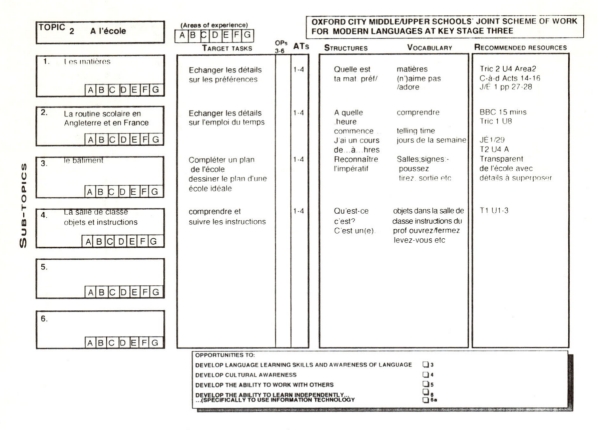

Figure 8

This approach may seem at variance with the apparent intention of the National Curriculum statutory document which lists attainment targets and statements of attainment before proceeding to programmes of study, but we came to accept that no assessment or recording procedure could have any meaning if it were not underpinned by a framework which helped teachers to work to defined objectives. The remainder of this book deals with how the system summarised in Chapter 1 could be adapted to serve National Curriculum requirements.

3. Involving pupils in their own assessment and recording

One of the justifiable claims of the OCEA system was that it allowed pupils to record their own progress, to comment on their experiences of the course and reflect on their study skills. This principle is endorsed in the second issue listed by *Teacher assessment in practice*. To be allowed to record one's own progress is per se to be involved in the assessment process. It is also worthy of mention that self-assessment and peer assessment are acknowledged as playing their part. In *Modern foreign languages for ages 11-16* (7.13)(November 1990) it is stated that:

> 'Where teachers are constantly monitoring pupils' progress in oral work, peer and self-assessment, as elements of non-statutory assessment, form an important part of the evidence at teacher's disposal. Some self-assessment is, indeed, required by our programmes of study.'

This implies not only the motivational value to pupils of self-assessment but the practical usefulness to teachers of providing supplementary evidence.

This is a point at which we can consider profiling as a way of serving several needs. As in the scheme described in *Recording progress*, we can use a profile form to provide information for pupils about the coming unit of study and set appropriate communicative targets as planned in the programme of study. As these targets are met, pupils can record their own attainment in consultation with the teacher. The profile document serves as a constant reminder of what the current work in the modern language is about and can invite pupils to reflect on their developing study skills, record new grammar points they have encountered and describe learning methods (group and individualised work, use of various technologies) they have experienced in the classroom and at home.

The profile completed by the teacher for a given unit of work can therefore contain, for the pupil's information, all the relevant topics and communicative targets set out in the corresponding section of the programme of study. It might include a checklist of the areas of experience covered in the unit. The model shown overleaf (figure 9) has these features, together with space for the pupil to record the highest level attained in each attainment target, and to record learning experiences, linguistic advances and his or her sense of development as a language learner.

```
┌─────────────────────────────────────────────────────────┐
│   NATIONAL CURRICULUM IN MODERN FOREIGN LANGUAGES       │
│          The Tennyson Upper Comprehensive School        │
│   Profile of attainment of [          ]                 │
│   Language Teacher [     ]     Tutor group [   ]        │
│   Language [   ] Unit [ ] Topic [         ]             │
│   Areas of experience covered by Topic  A B C D E F G   │
│   Description of tasks for each Attainment target       │
│                                             Highest level
│                                                attained │
│   AT 1 Listening                              [ ]       │
│   AT 2 Speaking                               [ ]       │
│   AT 3 Reading                                [ ]       │
│   AT 4 Writing                                [ ]       │
│   New language points learnt                            │
│   Comments on the unit: learning methods, use of        │
│       equipment, successes, difficulties)               │
│   Pupil's signature..........................           │
│   Teacher's signature........................           │
└─────────────────────────────────────────────────────────┘
```

Figure 9

Their accumulated observations on profiles would provide pupils with relevant comments for their contribution to the summative review sheet (report) dealt with in Chapter 6. Another treatment of the profile format might be to use the document as an end of unit certificate - useful where pupils have experience of a local graded objectives scheme. This could apply at school level or perhaps carry an LEA endorsement.

I have included the profile form because it is already a feature of many schemes designed to involve and motivate the learner through the assessment and recording process. Such a form obviously has some limitations. There will only be room for brief comment and such comment will tend to be towards the end of a unit, rather than an ongoing record of regular language learning. It is therefore worth also considering a diary format for recording. Such a diary could be kept either by individuals or by groups of pupils and could either be structured (e.g. by page layout) to ensure that pupils kept a well-balanced record, or open-ended to allow comment on what seemed to be most important at a particular time. Furthermore, such a record could be kept in the target language with suitable linguistic support from the teacher. Since much of the language used for this specialised diary would be reused regularly, pupils would have frequent opportunities to become familiar with it. This diary could accompany the accumulated **evidence** of pupils' achievement.

4. Coping with continuous assessment

Continuous assessment ought not to be confused with 'periodic assessment', e.g. end of unit tests commonly associated with GOML and assessment packs supplied with a number of published courses. It implies, as did the OCEA style of assessment described in Chapter 1, the regular application of defined criteria to the normal day-to-day work of pupils.

This is not to say that there could not be, should a teacher wish, a series of 'controlled tasks' integrated with the programme of study. This might prove a useful check on the authenticity of pupils' attainment, so long as it remained unobtrusive. However, teachers should **not** feel that they are failing in their duties by not including this element.

Good programmes will naturally contain activities which will offer pupils opportunities to demonstrate their developing skills, knowledge and understanding. It will not, however, be possible, given normal time constraints, to devise impeccable tasks which will guarantee at each stage of learning that each pupil will have opportunities simultaneously to perform all the statements of attainment relating to a given level of a given attainment target. Even if teachers **were** able to devise hundreds of tasks minutely matched with statements of attainment, one could be fairly sure that most pupils would either not satisfy some of the intended statements of attainment or in some cases greatly surpass them.

Activities likely to provide evidence of attainment are best devised and refined by a cyclical process of prediction of suitability and subsequent modification in the light of experience. If the teacher starts by devising an appropriate programme with learning paths to suit the needs of individual pupils, he or she should find **natural** opportunities to observe and assess pupils' performance in the attainment targets for the National Curriculum. Pupils may be taking part in oral work in pairs, collaboratively producing a brochure about their home town, working on an assignment at the listening post or filling in an evaluation form on their latest selection from the departmental reading library, to name but a few examples of assessable activities.

It is in the nature of the activities assessed in AT1 (Listening) and AT3 (Reading) that they are more likely to have a level of attainment **designed** into them, insofar as the teacher will select texts and devise tasks appropriate to the expected competence of pupils and mark on the basis of whether pupils did or did not carry out the task prescribed. This will obviously make the assessment easier since the teacher will know in advance what statements of attainment are relevant.

Activities planned for AT2 (Speaking) and AT4 (Writing) are more likely to be assessed by **outcome** since pupils may have more freedom regarding the language and content of their response to the task. Assessment by outcome is more demanding as there is a potentially greater range of statements of attainment which could come into play.

Collection of evidence

Not all activities will be equally easy to observe, assess and record. Some attainment targets will require different procedures from others, but what teachers will need to do is to ensure that there are manageable procedures for putting on record any measurable attainment as it is observed.

One can envisage a broad distinction between evidence which can be analysed at leisure - for example, completed listening and reading worksheets, exercise books, extended written project material and taped oral assignments which the teacher can take away - and evidence which is only transitory, available at the point of production, like unrecorded oral performance or forms of behaviour indicating 'understanding and responding' without recourse to writing.

AT1 (Listening)

This skill may be more often practised in class (using school-based recorders) or as a component of dialogue than as homework, although a number of teachers already offer pupils the chance to do listening activities in their own time. It may be typically assessed by worksheets with questions, matching activities or grids to fill with information. In the National Curriculum, the likely outcomes of planned tasks will need to be analysed so that teachers will have some idea of what success will mean in terms of statements of attainment. Apart from this new requirement, worksheet-based tasks can be marked whenever the teacher likes, presenting no classroom management problems.

Listening may also be assessed through the responses, verbal and non-verbal, of pupils engaged in conversation or carrying out instructions. In this case, teachers will need to evolve instant recording methods if the precious moment of attainment is not to be lost. More will be said about this under AT2.

AT2 (Speaking)

As with listening, speaking skills are most often assessed in the classroom though, again, pupils may use cassette recorders to record work at home. Teachers' main worry is about how to mark unrecorded speech of pupils. There seem to be two main problems here:

- the ephemeral nature of the attainment;

- the time demanded by the process.

CARRYING OUT INSTANT ASSESSMENT

Everything must be ready for the moment of performance, for there will be no time for elaborate descriptive notes to be made. Teachers will need to know the likely outcome of the task in terms of statements of attainment. They will also be increasingly aware of the likely performance of the pupils they are to listen to. Prescriptive tasks based on predictable situations will usually focus on a narrow range of statements, while open-ended tasks inviting, but not insisting upon, negotiation and sharing attitudes could leave the field wide open. Teachers must be aware of the practical limitations and design tasks which will leave them in control of the situation. They will need record sheets which minimise writing time. A possible National Curriculum mark sheet layout is illustrated and explained on pages 24-26.

NOT LETTING ASSESSMENT TAKE OVER FROM TEACHING

I have already said that we must not be intimidated by a false perception of National Curriculum continuous assessment. So, too, must we keep the role of oral assessment in perspective. It was never the intention of the Working Group on modern foreign languages that teachers should periodically conduct the equivalent of a full-scale GCSE oral with their language classes. There is no requirement that all pupils should be assessed in every week or even every month of their programme of study; nor are we told that they should be assessed in the context of every one of the seven areas of experience.

This means that there is no obligation to assess whole classes within prescribed weeks or units of study. Teachers drawing up an oral assessment schedule could for example target five pupils per week of a six-week cycle. This would allow every pupil in an average class at least six opportunities to demonstrate their progress in a school year. At the earlier stages, the tasks observed might take less than a minute, while even high achievers would provide adequate evidence of their progress in two or three minutes.

The supervision of pupils not being assessed can be taken care of by incorporating a periodic carousel session into the weekly routine and concentrating on the oral work corner.

We must not overlook, either, the variety of modes of assessment at our disposal. Here are just a few examples:

- Pupil-pupil role-play or dialogue (teacher or FLA marks either on the spot or from audio/video recording, or pupils mark each other).
- Pupil-teacher role-play or dialogue.
- Pupil-FLA role-play or dialogue.
- Teacher marks pupil during whole class questioning.
- Teacher or pupils mark presentation by groups or individuals.
- Teacher marks 'dossier sonore' made by pupil(s).

It will be evident that some of these can be used to ring the changes on 'teacher-on-the-spot' assessment and so further relieve the time constraints.

AT 2 (SPEAKING)

RANGE AND COMPLEXITY OF LANGUAGE AND TASKS	LEVEL	INDEPENDENCE AND SPONTANEITY	LEVEL	QUALITY OF COMMUNICATION
Respond very briefly / initiate	1		1	Approximate pronunciation and intonation
Respond using memorised language /express feelings likes and dislikes in simple terms	3	Initiate (and respond) adapt memorised words and phrases	3	
Initiate and respond in conversation and role play Use appropriate forms of personal address, offer simple explanations	4	Give a short presentation or prompted talk	4	
Give and seek information about past, present and future actions and events	6	Initiate and sustain an unprompted conversation (with an element of unpredictability) Ask for and offer explanations about meanings	6	
				(LEVEL 7) Speak with fluency, good intonation and little error on familiar topics
Discuss facts, ideas, experiences, using range of language	8	Initiate/maintain conversation with unfamiliar people or unpredictable elements	8	

Figure 10

AT3 (Reading)

A skill which can be exercised at school or at home, reading may be intensive (specific comprehension tasks testing understanding of gist or detail) or extensive (pupils choosing reading material and keeping a log of their own progress and reactions). Note that the ability to choose appropriate reading material is in itself a characteristic of attainment in the National Curriculum. Pupils may also provide evidence of their progress in reading through their response to written instructions and teachers will occasionally want to record such a response as it happens.

AT4 (Writing)

Writing provides the most lasting and tangible evidence of the four attainment targets. Where the National Curriculum differs from traditional forms of assessment is in recognising that the redrafting of existing written work to achieve greater accuracy and coherence is a skill in its own right. Teachers have already discovered the potential of the word processor for storage of previous work and its redrafting. No doubt, too, the text editing powers of the word processor can be exploited by the most able pupils to adapt existing texts to new registers.

AT 4 (WRITING)

RANGE AND COMPLEXITY OF LANGUAGE AND TASKS	LEVEL	INDEPENDENCE AND CREATIVITY	LEVEL	ACCURACY OF COMMUNICATION
Copy familiar words	1		1	copy correctly
Write short sentences - Copy a range of characters(Ch & J)	3	Write short phrases from memory	3	
Convey simple information or feelings - Copy a wide range of characters(Ch & J)	4	Write a small number of related sentences from memory - adapt a simple text by substituting simple words and set phrases	4	
Write about familair topics and experiences, including future & past events using simple descriptive language	6		6	(LEVEL 7) Give clear instructions Redraft to achieve greater accuracy, precision, variety of expression
Write a short imaginative text - Seek information or the view of others on a matter of personal significance	8	Develop the content of something something read, seen or heard - Express ideas or opinions on a familiar topic	8	

Figure 11

The interpreting of evidence

All work done under the heading of one or more of the attainment targets must be viewed through the magnifying glass of the statements of attainment. Teachers are understandably apprehensive about calling to mind at a moment's notice any group of up to four out of 102 statements when they mark pupils' work. Some reassurances are in order.

★ At the early stages of key stage 3, pupils will only be operating over a very limited range of statements of attainment and repeated application of these should bring rapid familiarity with the lower levels before new ground has to be broken.

★ There are techniques for getting our minds around the full range of statements:

- 'bracketing' the levels into groups with which we develop a broad familiarity, for example by association with categories of learner (see Pathfinder 12, *Progressing through the attainment targets* by Ian Lane);

- 'targeting' certain key levels and becoming very familiar with their statements of attainment so that they can act as landmarks to higher and lower attainments;

- understanding the principles underlying the different strands of attainment, as illustrated by pages D6-D9 of the NSG (simplified versions of two of these charts are shown in figures 10 and 11).

If assessment tasks are integrated into programmes of study suitable for the pupils in question, teachers should have some idea of the outcomes they can expect. Pupils will probably not fulfil whole sets of statements of attainment in a given task, but may more typically satisfy one or two. Their attainment may even span more than one level, e.g. achieving statement of attainment (a) for level 3 and statement of attainment (c) for level 4. At the point of observation and assessment, then, teachers need a suitably designed sheet to enable them to record features of pupils' attainment as quickly and conveniently as possible.

5. Recording pupils' performance

Figure 12 shows one way of recording individual achievements in terms of statements of attainment without having to waste undue space on accommodating all ten levels on any given page of the mark book.

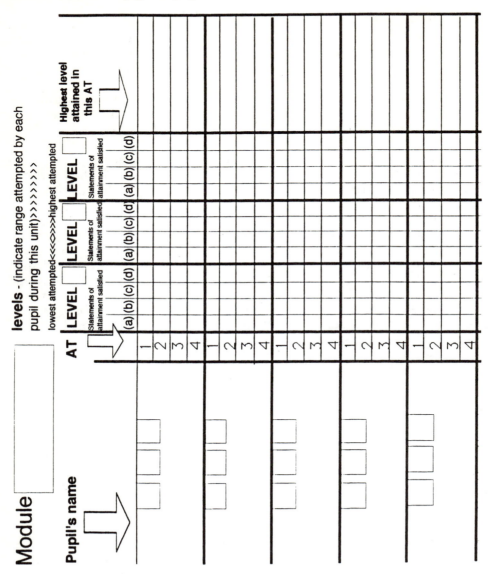

Figure 12

Figures 13(a) and (b) show two approaches to using this ruling. In (a) we assume, for example, a beginners' class with little expected variation in the level of attainment. In this case, the three selected levels (wide vertical columns) can be the same for all pupils. In the example given, any statement of attainment ticked in the first column would relate to level 1 of each attainment target (listed 1, 2, 3 and 4 for each pupil entry box) and ticks in the second and third columns would relate to levels 2 and 3.

Reality is often more complex, and in (b) we see a way of 'customising' each pupil entry box so that the left-hand column refers to the lowest expected level for that pupil (L), the middle column to the next level up (M) and the right-hand column to a yet higher level (H) should the pupil attain it in that unit of work. By using this method, we can cater for all the expected attainments within a reasonable time period of a mixed-ability class.

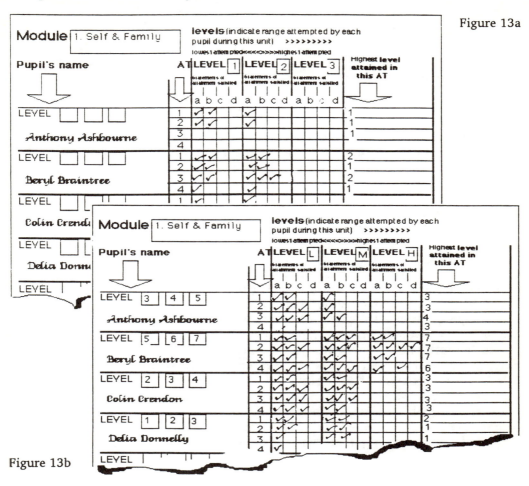

Figure 13a

Figure 13b

Figure 14 is provided to clarify the functions of each part of the mark sheet.

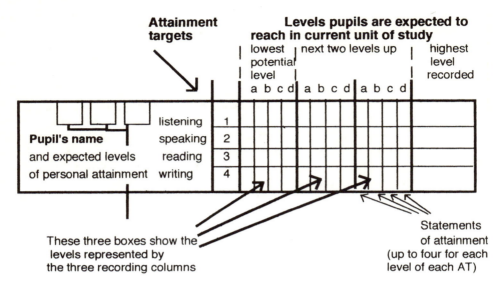

Figure 14

Equipped with a mark sheet of this or comparable design, the teacher is able to record with a stroke of the pen each statement of attainment as it is satisfied by the pupil's performance, whether in the midst of a lesson or after school while marking workbooks.

When to record that statements of attainment have been completed raises the question of what constitutes acceptable evidence of performance. The recent SEAC booklet, *Teacher assessment at key stage 3 - modern foreign languages* (see page 11) gives an official but flexible answer, namely that we are professionals in the business of teaching and assessment and that we should exercise our professional judgment in deciding whether the pupil 'can' behave linguistically as the operative statement of attainment indicates. For some other subjects it has been suggested that a statement of attainment should be fulfilled on at least two occasions. We would certainly expect there to be an element of **reliability** in pupils' performance, consistent with ability to replicate that performance. In practice, we might need to see or hear one pupil's performance several times before we are convinced, given our knowledge of their learning capacity, that they could cope, while with another we might be perfectly confident with one piece of evidence. (An advantage of basing our judgment on naturally occurring coursework is that we see pupils engaged in their day-to-day performance, rather than artificially parroting items they have 'mugged up' for a test.)

6. Reporting progress through a periodic review sheet

While the pupil profile can be valuable in giving the pupil advance information about the unit of study and allowing him or her to be involved in the recording process, there is still a need for a more formal document for circulation at times of the year determined on a whole school basis and in conjunction with other subject reports. Figure 15 shows a possible layout for such a review sheet. Apart from the obvious spaces for pupil's names, forms and teacher's names, this prototype accommodates topics studied since the last report, together with areas of experience which those topics have 'explored'. There follows a grid for recording the levels reached in each attainment target assessed since last time.

The Edward VIII Academy

Review of the progress of ☐
Year ☐
Language teacher ☐ Tutor ☐
Language ☐

Attainment targets	Levels attained	List of topics studied	AoE
1 (Listening)			
2 (Speaking)			
3 (Reading)			
4 (Writing)			

Pupil's self-evaluation and response to the course

Teacher's overall assessment

Parent's response to the assessment

Figure 15

Teachers may wish to devise ways of making the meanings of the attainment target levels clearer to readers of the review. There are some problems here. Time will not permit teachers to write in the statements of attainment which relate to the level achieved and space might also prove a problem. For those schools geared to writing reviews by computer-generated statement banks it should be a simple enough matter to key-code sets of statements for each level of the attainment target. Otherwise, the only way of offering the full description of any performance would be to issue a chart of all the statements of attainment to every parental home. But when the statements are printed, will they mean anything to the reader unless (s)he is conversant with the jargon which permeates the statements of attainment? How many 'consumers' of the review will instantly visualise the pupil who can 'initiate and sustain an unprompted conversation...'? This is not to deride the language used: it is succinct and plain, but it depends on professional experience for full understanding. Teachers might explore ways of expressing what it means to be a 'level x speaker' so that parents can recognise their children as a linguist, rather than a machine!

Most teachers would probably agree that such a review should contain freer, more open-ended statements to supplement the rigid objectivity of National Curriculum statements of attainment. I have therefore incorporated spaces for comment by pupils, teachers and parents.

- The pupil's comment could include:

    ★ responses to the learning methods used (e.g. collaborative and independent activities and use of various types of technology;

    ★ comments on their developing study skills;

    ★ comments on most and least enjoyed aspects of the units studied with corresponding requests for guidance.

- The teachers' statement might be used to clarify the levels attained (see problem above) or to offer advice on the pupil's further progress.

- The parental response box should give space for more than a mere signature of receipt.

The entire process from planning the integration of teaching with assessment to the issuing of progress reviews to parents is illustrated by figure 16.

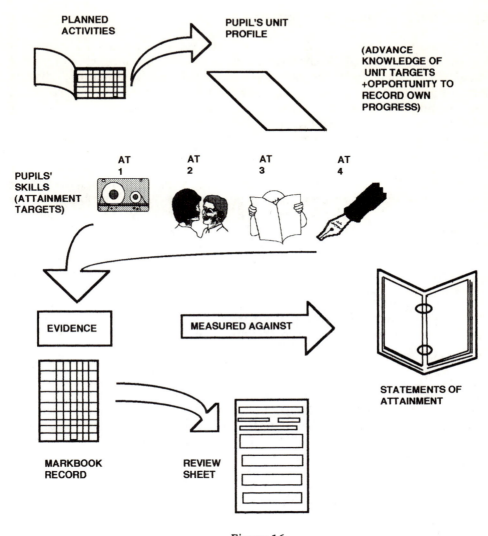

Figure 16

7. Recapitulation and conclusions

Keeping assessment in proportion

In the course of the book, I have re-examined the principles applied in the scheme which forms the basis of *Recording progress*. I hope to have shown that the National Curriculum requirements are compatible with much of what was proposed in this earlier book. I have attempted to predict what form continuous assessment might take within the National Curriculum framework. I hope that I have demonstrated that it should not, indeed must not, obstruct or usurp the teaching process. For the teacher it should not entail a dramatic departure from accepted practice.

What **is** new, I have acknowledged, is the application to that practice of more detailed criteria than have previously been required. Herein probably lie most teachers' perceived problems. We have looked at several approaches to assimilating the statements of attainment and I hope that these may help the reader towards a clearer view of them. Tricks of memorisation are, however, no substitute for the experience that comes from applying the statements to actual examples of pupils' work and discussing interpretations with other teachers. With the benefit of practical experience and the help of such guidance as the excellent 'Dulux' charts (pp D6-D9) of the NSG, teachers should quickly gain confidence about the general feel of pupils' performance in relation to the attainment target levels so that they need recourse to the statements of attainment for fine-tuning only.

To turn to the recording aspect, we have all detected a certain cynicism ('If it moves, assess it') among our colleagues in other subjects. Lest my suggestion for a mark book layout (see pages 24-26) be taken as an incitement to 'education by tick-list', I should perhaps emphasise at this point that forms and charts should be the servants and not the masters of the assessor. A few reminders and reassurances should not come amiss here.

- There are not always as many as four statements of attainment per AT level; some have only two related statements.

- You don't have to assess/record the full range of skills (ATs) for every pupil in every study unit of your programme. What matters is that you assess often enough to keep pace with each pupil's development so that your record as nearly as possible reflects pupils' latest attainments.

- There is not a minimum required number of successful attempts at a task before you are allowed to record success. If you are confident, through your personal familiarity with the pupil, that (s)he has acquired the knowledge, skill and understanding necessary to satisfy the statement of attainment in question, you are professionally justified in recording this fact.

This is not to understate difficulties. The last of these reassurances raises the vexed question of what constitutes effective learning and how it is apparent to the teacher. It is not entirely an abdication of responsibility to say that this problem is not peculiar to the National Curriculum. There are a number of acknowledged levels of effectiveness of learning. We might say of a pupil: 'succeeded on that occasion'; or 'tends to succeed'; or even 'can be expected to succeed in two years' time'.

There remain a number of required aspects of learning in the National Curriculum which have not yet received due attention. In our brief look at programmes of study design, we saw that sections 3-6 of the programmes of study should be planned for. Likewise, we must cater for the cross-curricular aspects of language learning.

While it might be tempting for the sake of tidiness to incorporate all conceivable aspects of the National Curriculum into pupil profiles and mark books, it becomes clear that we would soon find ourselves confronted with the worst of all possible tick-lists if we were to do so. If our purpose in keeping records is to provide evidence that we have incorporated all desired features into our programmes of study, then it is in the programmes that enquirers ought to look first. The OCEA model (and this is but one of an increasing number of examples worth consideration) allows the planner to indicate where the requirements of sections 3-6 are being fulfilled.

By allowing pupils to record their learning experiences, either at the end of a unit on their personal profiles or as a daily or weekly diary as already suggested, we can also pick up whether pupils are getting the experiences required by the Statutory Order (e.g. 'My speaking was assessed through role-play and I was asked to redraft my written assignment using a computer'). Both programmes of study sections 3-6 and the many cross-curricular aspects can be referred to in the unit plan, in individual lesson plans and in feedback from pupils without the teacher having to make separate reference to these in the daily recording progress.

Making the system serve real needs

Whereas *Recording progress* described an established working system, this book has entered the more dangerous territory of attempting to predict imminent needs and suggesting ways of meeting them. However, while the reality of a year or two hence may diverge slightly from these projections I am confident that the above principles will largely continue to apply.

My final recommendation is that practising teachers, should they wish to follow the suggestions I have made, should **adapt** my models to fit their particular circumstances, rather than simply **copy** them. Patterns should exist for guidance only, or they will become a straightjacket. There is considerable scope for changes of layout in recording documents and for the omission or addition of steps in the process. The extent of pupil involvement in the recording process may vary considerably. Some teachers will wish to stay with familiar systems, only adapting marginally to incorporate these ideas.

What matters in the end is that teachers, pupils, parents and other interested parties have quick and regular access to the ever-growing picture of the progress of the young language learner. If this book goes some way to facilitating that access, it will have achieved its end.

Hoping to find an alternative to the overused 'tablets of stone' metaphor in disclaiming divine wisdom, I came recently upon the German saying '*Dies ist nicht das Ei von Kolumbus*'. May you 'lay' and 'hatch' your own plans successfully.